Draw Your Own Encyclopaedia

Scotland's Seabirds

In Association With The *Scottish Seabird Centre*

Colin M. Drysdale

Illustrated by ______________________________

Pictish Beast Publications

ISBN - 978-1-909832-59-6

Published by Pictish Beast Publications, Glasgow, UK.
Published in the United Kingdom
First Printing: 2018. First Edition.

www.PictishBeastPublications.com

How To Use This Book

This is a *Draw Your Own Encyclopaedia* book for children aged six to twelve. It will provide you with interesting introductions to a variety of different aspects of the lives of Scotland's seabirds, along with quick facts, questions you can answer and, at the end, a pop quiz where you can test the knowledge you have gained by reading this book. So far, this may seem like any other book of facts, but unlike almost every other such book, you are allowed to draw in this one. In fact, you are actively encouraged to do so! Through this, you will become the illustrator of your very own encyclopaedia chapter all about the different seabird species that call Scotland home.

When adding your own pictures to this book, it is important that you seek out suitable images to base your own ones on. This can be done either by consulting other books, or by entering an appropriate search term into an internet search engine (such as *Google*). If you choose to use an internet search engine, the best results will usually be achieved by entering the bird's name followed by the words *Bird* and *Picture*. For example, for the illustration on page four, the best search term to use would be *Northern Gannet Bird Picture*.

For Parents And Educators

To help ensure your child's safety online, please use appropriate online safety procedures and supervise their internet usage at all times when looking for pictures on which they can base their illustrations for this book. You can also use this time to discuss internet safety with your child, as well as strategies for searching for specific information, and how to decide whether information they find on the internet is reliable or not.

If you wish to use any of the contents of this book for educational purposes, an educational licence (which allows you to legally photocopy pages to create handouts) can be purchased from *www.pictishbeastpublications.com/draw-your-own-encyclopaedi*a. Ideas for classroom activities to accompany this book can also be accessed through this webpage.

What Is A Seabird?

A seabird is any bird species that is specifically adapted for life in the marine environment. They tend to live longer, breed later and have fewer offspring than other birds. Many seabird species also nest in large colonies and undertake long migrations. While some seabirds live close to the coast, others live far out to sea, and some may not touch dry land for several years in a row. However, all seabirds must return to shore to breed, and it is during this time (known as the breeding season) that we have the best opportunity to see them and learn more about them.

Quick Fact: One group of seabirds, the Procellariiforms or tubenoses, have a tube along the top of their beak. This adaptation gives them a much better sense of smell than almost all other bird species and they use this to help them find food in the vastness of the ocean.

With a wing span of up to 180 centimetres, the largest Scottish seabird is the northern gannet. Draw a picture of a northern gannet in flight here, showing its long narrow wings that are an adaptation for flying long distances to find food.

Quick Fact: While gannets and other species that fly great distances to find food have long narrow wings, those that dive deep underwater have shorter, stubbier wings.

Quick Fact: Many seabirds have waterproof feathers that protect them from getting cold and wet, and almost all of them have webbed feet to help them swim.

How Many Species Of Seabird Live In Scotland?

Twenty-four different species regularly breed in Scotland. These include species such as the puffin, the common guillemot, the razorbill, the Manx shearwater, the European storm petrel and the herring gull. For some species, Scotland is home to the majority of the world's population. For example, around eighty percent of the world's northern gannets and sixty percent of great skuas nest in Scotland. This makes Scotland one of the most important places in the world for seabirds.

Quick Fact: Many seabirds are drawn to Scotland because of its highly productive seas, and the availability of many remote cliffs and islands where they can nest. These inaccessible locations help keep them, and their chicks, safe from predators.

Can you name three species of seabird that regularly breed in Scotland?

1.
2.
3.

Scotland is home to over half of the world's great skuas. This species is a kleptoparasite, meaning it steals food from other seabirds, such as gulls, terns and gannets. Draw a picture of a great skua chasing another seabird to steal its food.

How Can You Identify Different Seabird Species?

Each seabird species has a unique body size, shape and colouration, and you can use these features to tell different species apart. For example, northern gannets are large white birds with long narrow wings tipped with black. In contrast, greater black-backed gulls have white bodies and black wings, while European storm petrels are tiny dark brown birds with a white rump. Finally, common guillemots are plump birds with white bodies, and black backs and heads.

Quick Fact: Identifying seabirds is made more complicated by the fact that young birds may be a very different colour from adults, and adults may have different plumage in summer and winter. However, the body size and shape always remains the same.

Some seabirds also have very different beak shapes, which can help you identify them. For example, common guillemots have narrow pointed beaks, while their close relatives, the razorbills, have thick blunt beaks. Draw the heads of a common guillemot and a razorbill here to show how their beaks differ in shape.

Quick Fact: Both common guillemots and razorbills feed on small fish. However, because of their different beak shapes, common guillemots can only catch fish one at a time, while razorbills can hold several fish in their beaks at once.

What Is A Seabird Colony?

A seabird colony is an area where many individual birds come together to nest. Sometimes they are all the same species, but in many cases, many different seabirds will come together to nest in the same colony. The location of a colony is often selected because it is close to a good supply of food for feeding their young. Seabird colonies also tend to be inaccessible to ground-based predators, like cats, foxes and rats, which might eat their eggs and chicks. This means that many seabird colonies are found on steep coastal cliffs or on remote islands that are naturally free from predators.

Quick Fact: Puffins on the island of Ailsa Craig on Scotland's west coast were virtually wiped out when rats arrived there in the late 1800s. They only returned once the rats were eliminated from the island in 1991.

While seabird colonies can seem very disorganised, they are actually very cleverly arranged. Different bird species occupy different levels in a colony, and each nest is spaced out to avoid conflict between neighbours. Find a picture of a seabird colony and see if you can spot the organised patterns in amongst the seemingly chaotic mass of birds, then draw a picture of it here.

How Many Northern Gannets Nest On The Bass Rock?

The Bass Rock is one of the largest seabird colonies in Scotland, and since it is only a short distance from Edinburgh, it is also one of the easiest to visit. Each Spring, about half a million seabirds return to the Bass Rock and its neighbouring islands in the Firth of Forth. This includes 150,000 northern gannets which nest on the Bass Rock itself. This is almost half of all the northern gannets in the world. In fact, there are so many of them on the Bass Rock that their nests almost completely cover the entire surface of this long-extinct volcano.

Quick Fact: The Bass Rock is so famous for its northern gannets that the scientific name for the species, *Morus bassanus*, comes from the island's name!

How many gannets return each year to nest on the Bass Rock?

Find a picture of the Bass Rock and examine it closely to see if you can spot the tens of thousands of northern gannets that cover almost its entire surface during the breeding season. Their white bodies make the island look like it's capped with snow. Draw a picture of the Bass Rock here.

What Do Seabirds Eat?

Seabirds eat a wide range of marine animals including fish, squid and crustaceans (such as crabs). In fact, many seabirds will eat almost anything they can catch. Some species, like storm petrels, will pick small pieces of food off the surface of the sea, while others, like puffins and guillemots, will dive deep underwater in search of fish. When foraging, seabirds can travel long distances, and some may travel hundreds of kilometres in search of food. They will often feed along side other marine predators, such as whales, dolphins, porpoises and seals.

Quick Fact: When feeding, puffins can dive to depths as deep as sixty metres on a single breath of air. That is more than twice the length of an average swimming pool!

Quick Fact: During a foraging trip, northern gannets will typically travel around 500 kilometres. However, the longest ever recorded was over 2,500 kilometres.

Northern gannets catch fish by plunging into the sea from as high as thirty metres in the air. See if you can find a video of this behaviour online, and then draw a picture here of a flock of northern gannets plunge-diving to catch fish.

Quick Fact: Hitting the water after a thirty metre dive is like hitting concrete, and northern gannets have a number of special adaptations to ensure they don't get hurt. This includes strong muscles in their necks and air sacs under their skin to cushion them from the impact. To stop water going up their noses, they also have no external nostrils!

How Long Do Seabirds Live?

Seabirds can live for a surprisingly long time. Puffins can live for twenty years, herring gulls over thirty years and northern gannets for thirty-five years. However, the longest-lived species in Scotland is the fulmar. Scientists working at a seabird colony on the island of Eynhallow in Orkney regularly saw the same fulmar between 1951 and 1996. It was probably around sixty-eight years old when it was last seen. In contrast, most of the birds you see in your garden or local park will live for less than five years, and very few will survive for more than ten.

Quick Fact: As well as living for a long time, seabirds also take a long time to mature. While land birds will often breed when they are just a year old, many seabirds will not start breeding until they are five or six years old.

Fulmars are amongst the longest-lived of all seabirds in the world. Draw a picture of a fulmar sitting on its nest here, and write down how old the oldest recorded fulmar was thought to have been when it was last seen.

Quick Fact: Many seabirds mate for life. This means that when they return to their breeding colony each spring, they reunite with the same partner they mated with the year before.

Quick Fact: Most seabirds return to the same colony where they were born. However, some adventurous individuals will try new locations, and this is how new seabird colonies are formed.

Where Do Seabirds Go In Winter?

While seabird colonies are a hive of activity during the summer breeding season, in the winter they can appear almost completely deserted. So where do all the birds go? While some will move to different sea areas around Scotland, others travel to more distant places. Some Scottish puffins spend the winter in the Bay of Biscay (which is between France and Spain), while Manx shearwaters fly to South America. However, the longest distances are covered by Arctic terns. After leaving their breeding colonies in Scotland, they fly as far south as the Antarctic before returning the following Spring.

Quick Fact: During their lives, each Arctic tern will fly up to 2.4 million kilometres. This is the same distance as making three trips from the Earth to the Moon and back again!

How far will Arctic terns fly in their life times?

Despite their small size, Arctic terns undertake the longest migrations of any animal species, and each year they will travel up to seventy thousand kilometres. Draw a picture of an Arctic tern here.

Have Any Scottish Seabirds Gone Extinct?

Unfortunately, the answer to this question is yes. There was a species called the great auk that used to nest in Scotland, but it became extinct about 170 years ago. Great auks were related to puffins, guillemots and razorbills, but at up to 85 centimetres tall, they were much larger. The only time great auks left the water was to breed. Great auks used to nest along many Scottish coasts, but the last colonies here were on St Kilda and Papa Westray in Orkney. The final pair of great auks were killed in Iceland in 1844.

Quick Fact: Great auks are sometimes referred to as the 'penguins of the North'. This is because, like penguins, they were so well adapted to swimming in the sea that they had lost the ability to fly. This made it easy for humans to catch the great auks when they came ashore to breed, and hunting by humans is what led to their extinction.

Draw a picture of a great auk here, and write the year when it became extinct underneath.

What Threats Do Scottish Seabirds Face?

Scotland's seabirds face a wide variety of threats. These include becoming tangled in fishing gear, overfishing of their food, and swallowing bits of plastic. However, for many Scottish seabirds, the greatest threat they face is from climate change. During the breeding season, seabird species, such as puffins, rely on a small fish called a sandeel to feed themselves and their growing chicks. Unfortunately, as the seas around Scotland warm, sandeels will become increasingly rare. This will mean that very little food will be available for seabirds or their chicks.

Quick Fact: Almost all seabirds have plastics in their stomachs. One fulmar from the North Sea had over 1,500 pieces of plastic in its stomach, while another had over twenty grams of plastic in it. This is the same as a human having two kilograms of plastic clogging their guts.

During the breeding season, puffins catch sandeels and carry them back to their burrows to feed their chicks. As a result of climate change, sandeels will become much rarer, leaving little food for puffins to feed to their chicks. Draw a picture of a puffin standing at the entrance to its burrow with a beakful of sandeels.

Can you name three other threats faced by Scottish seabirds?

1.

2.

3.

How Can We Help Protect Scotland's Seabirds?

Everyone can play their part in helping to protect Scotland's seabirds. This can include only buying fish from sustainable sources that do their best not to harm seabirds or the marine environment, and joining a marine conservation organisation. In addition, if we reduced the number of disposable straws, bags and other plastic items that we use, fewer of them will end up in the sea where they are swallowed by seabirds and other marine life. While each individual person's contribution may seem very small, when combined with the efforts of many others, all these small actions can end up having a big impact.

Name three things you can do to help protect Scotland's seabirds:

1.

2.

3.

See if you can come up with an idea for a poster which would encourage people to help protect Scotland's seabirds. Draw a picture of your poster design here.

Pop Quiz

The answers to all these questions can be found elsewhere in this book. See if you can answer them all!

1. What is a seabird?
2. How many species of seabird regularly breed in Scotland?
3. What is Scotland's largest seabird?
4. How can you tell different seabird species apart?
5. What is a seabird colony?
6. How old was the oldest recorded fulmar?
7. To what depth can a puffin dive?
8. What is the longest foraging trip recoded for a northern gannet?
9. Can you name the flightless seabird that used to live in Scotland, but that is now extinct?
10. How far do Arctic terns fly each year?
11. How many northern gannets nest on the Bass Rock?
12. What type of fish do puffins rely on to feed their chicks?
13. What shape of beak do razorbills have?
14. How many seabirds nest on the Bass Rock and its neighbouring islands in the Firth of Forth each year?
15. Can you name three threats that Scottish seabirds face?

Write Your Answers Here:

1. ________________________________
2. ________________________________
3. ________________________________
4. ________________________________
5. ________________________________
6. ________________________________
7. ________________________________
8. ________________________________
9. ________________________________
10. ________________________________
11. ________________________________
12. ________________________________
13. ________________________________
14. ________________________________
15. ________________________________

Pop Quiz – The Answers

1. A seabird is any bird that is adapted for living in the marine environment.
2. Twenty four species of seabird regularly breed in Scotland.
3. With a wing span of up to 180 centimetres, Scotland's largest seabird is the northern gannet.
4. Different seabird species can be told apart by their size, shape and colouration.
5. A seabird colony is an area where many seabirds come together to breed, and a single colony can have half a million or more birds in it.
6. The oldest recorded age for a fulmar is sixty-eight years.
7. Puffins can stay underwater for up to one minute and during this time, they can dive as deep as sixty metres.
8. The longest foraging trip recorded for a northern gannet was over 2,500 kilometres long!
9. The flightless bird that used to live in Scotland, but that is now extinct, is the great auk. It looked similar to a penguin, but it was more closely related to puffins, razorbills and guillemots.
10. Arctic terns spend their summer months in Scotland and other northern countries, but after they have finished breeding, they migrate as far south as Antarctica before returning north in the following Spring. During this time, they can travel up to 70,000 kilometres.
11. Each summer, the Bass Rock is home to around 150,000 nesting northern gannets!
12. In Scotland, puffins rely on a small fish called a sandeel to feed their chicks.
13. Razorbills have thick blunt beaks. Unlike the narrow pointed beaks of the closely related black guillemots, this beak shape allows them to hold several small fish at once.
14. Each year, approximately half a million seabirds nest on these islands.
15. Threats faced by Scottish seabirds include the ingestion of plastics, overfishing of their prey, getting tangled in fishing gear and climate change.

Where To Find Out More About Scotland's Seabirds

If you would like to learn more about the seabird species that live in Scotland, and other parts of the world, you can check out the following resources:

- **Scottish Seabird Centre:** The *Scottish Seabird Centre* is based in North Berwick, and is one of the best places to visit if you wish to see a real live seabird colony. You can find out more about it at *www.seabird.org*.
- **Seabird Webcams:** If you cannot visit the *Scottish Seabird Centre* in person, you can still see what seabird colonies are all about through the centre's network of webcams at *seabird.org/wildlife/webcams/12/28*.
- **Seabird Conservation:** You can find out about the work being done by the *Scottish Seabird Centre* to help conserve seabirds and other marine life at *seabird.org/conservation/44*.
- **Seabird Biology:** You can find out more about the biology of seabirds in general at *en.wikipedia.org/wiki/Seabird*.

About The *Scottish Seabird Centre* (*SSC*)

The *Scottish Seabird Centre* (*SSC*) is a conservation and education charity based in North Berwick on the east coast of Scotland. It is dedicated to inspiring people to care for wildlife and the natural environment. It is a non-profit making visitor attraction, meaning that the income generated by visitors is invested in the charitable work undertaken by its committed team of staff and volunteers.

Help Support The *Scottish Seabird Centre*

You can help support the *Scottish Seabird Centre* in a number of different ways, including:

- **Becoming a member:** By becoming a member, you not only get free entry to the *Discovery Centre*, you also get discounts on boat trips, and purchases from the gift shop.
- **Wildlife Adoptions:** You can adopt seals, puffins or gannet families through the *SSC*. Each adoption pack includes a soft toy of the sponsored animal, a personalised adoption certificate, an A5 poster and a factsheet. In addition, details of your adoption will be displayed in the *SSC's Discovery Centre*.
- **Volunteering:** *SSC* volunteers have a wide range of ages and abilities. Some volunteer once a month and some a few hours a week. No matter how much time you have to offer, or what you would like to do, the *SSC* would love to hear from you.
- **Donating:** The *SSC* is a registered charity, and every penny it receives is invested in the education and conservation work they do, so your donation will make a real difference to seabirds in Scotland.

To find out more, please visit *seabird.org/visit/support/10/24*

Dedication

This book is dedicated to all who love seabirds, learning and drawing, regardless of their age!

Books available now in the *Draw Your Own Encyclopaedia* series from Pictish Beast Publications:

1. **Mammals** - ISBN: 978-1-909832-39-8. RRP: UK: £6.99 US: $8.99.
2. **Birds** - ISBN: 978-1-909832-41-1. RRP: UK: £6.99 US: $8.99.
3. **Reptiles** - ISBN: 978-1-909832-42-8. RRP: UK: £6.99 US: $8.99.
4. **Amphibians** - ISBN: 978-1-909832-43-5. RRP: UK: £6.99 US: $8.99.
5. **Fish** - ISBN: 978-1-909832-44-2. RRP: UK: £6.99 US: $8.99.
6. **Invertebrates** - ISBN: 978-1-909832-45-9. RRP: UK: £6.99 US: $8.99.
7. **Animals Box Set** - ISBN: 978-1-909832-51-0. RRP: UK: £39.99 US:$49.99.
8. **Scotland's Dolphins** - ISBN: 978-1-909832-55-8. RRP: UK: £6.99 US: $8.99.
9. **Scotland's Seabirds** - ISBN: 978-1-909832-59-6. RRP: UK: £6.99 US: $8.99.

Books coming soon in the *Draw Your Own Encyclopaedia* series:

1. **Scotland's Native Wildlife** - ISBN: 978-1-909832-59-6. RRP: UK: £6.99 US: $8.99.
2. **Scotland's Castles** - ISBN: 978-1-909832-62-6. RRP: UK: £6.99 US: $8.99.
3. **Scotland's Folklore** - ISBN: 978-1-909832-63-3. RRP: UK: £6.99 US: $8.99.
4. **Planet Earth** - ISBN: 978-1-909832-46-6. RRP: UK: £6.99 US: $8.99.
5. **Our Solar System** - ISBN: 978-1-909832-47-3. RRP: UK: £6.99 US: $8.99.
6. **Deep Space** - ISBN: 978-1-909832-48-0. RRP: UK: £6.99 US: $8.99.
7. **The Universe** - ISBN: 978-1-909832-49-7. RRP: UK: £6.99 US: $8.99.
8. **Space Exploration** - ISBN: 978-1-909832-50-3. RRP: UK: £6.99 US: $8.99.

For more information on this series of books (including a full list of available and upcoming titles), visit: *www.pictishbeastpublications.com/draw-your-own-encyclopaedia*

Lightning Source UK Ltd.
Milton Keynes UK
UKHW05f1000150918
328876UK00007B/17/P

9 781909 832596